SIMPLY**SCIENCE**

The Simple Science of

MAGNETS

by Emily James

CAPSTONE PRESS
a capstone imprint

A+ Books are published by Capstone Press,
1710 Roe Crest Drive, North Mankato, Minnesota 56003
www.mycapstone.com

Library of Congress Cataloging-in-Publication Data
Cataloging-in-publication information is on file with the Library of Congress.
ISBN 978-1-5157-7083-1 (library binding)
ISBN 978-1-5157-7090-9 (paperback)
ISBN 978-1-5157-7098-5 (eBook PDF)

Editorial Credits
Jaclyn Jaycox, editor; Jenny Bergstrom, designer; Jo Miller, media researcher; Tori Abraham, production specialist

Photo Credits
Getty Images: Visuals Unlimited, 20; iStockphoto: sturti, 26-27; Newscom: Digital Light/Richard Hutchings, 8, Universal Images Group/Dorling Kindersley, 14, 15; Science Source: Charles D. Winters, 9; Shutterstock: Algonga, 29 (sea turtle silhouette), Andrea Paggiaro, 21, AngelPet, 23 (inset), bikeriderlondon, 7 (inset), f-f-f-f, 11 (nail), Gerald Bernard, 24, Jan H Andersen, 10, Kawin Ounprasertsuk, 28, Malll Themd, 11 (paper clip), mangax, 12-13, Mega Pixel, 11 (magnet), Montri Thipsorn, 29 (inset), Olivier Le Moal, 4-5, optimarc, back cover (bottom), Peter Hermes Furian, 17 (inset), Pichet siritantiwat, 6-7, 28-29 (background), raduned, back cover (top), Sergey Nivens, 25, takasu, cover, Terrance Emerson, 18-19, Tyler Olson, 22-23, xtock, 16-17

Design Elements
Shutterstock: bikeriderlondon

Note to Parents, Teachers, and Librarians

This Simply Science book uses full color photographs and a nonfiction format to introduce the concept of magnets. *The Simple Science of Magnets* is designed to be read aloud to a pre-reader or to be read independently by an early reader. Photographs help listeners and early readers understand the text and concepts discussed. The book encourages further learning by including the following sections: Table of Contents, Glossary, Read More, Internet Sites, and Index. Early readers may need assistance using these features.

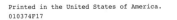

Printed in the United States of America.
010374F17

Table of CONTENTS

Magic Magnets

Magnets can make objects move—without touching them! When a string pulls something, you see it work.

But you can't see a magnet's power.
Magnets seem to move things by magic.

How Do Magnets Work?

A magnet has an invisible area around it.
The area is called a magnetic field. A magnet
can pull things that are in this area only.
Set a paper clip far away from a magnet.

Then slowly move the clip
closer. Suddenly it will zip toward
the magnet. Fast! The clip has entered the
magnet's magnetic field.

Magnets can't move all objects. They move
only special kinds of metal.

8

Steel and iron can be moved easily by a magnet. Copper and nickel cannot. Neither can cotton, rubber, or plastic.

steel

copper

Magnets can turn some metal objects into magnets. Try this: Hang an iron nail from the end of a magnet. Then touch a paper clip to the nail. What happens?

The clip sticks to the nail! The nail has
turned into a magnet. Now pull the nail
away from the magnet. Does the paper clip
still stick to the nail?

North and South Poles

Most magnets look like bars or horseshoes.

Their power is strongest at the two ends.

One end is called the north pole. The other end is the south pole. The poles can push as well as pull.

Poles that are alike push against each other.
They repel. The north pole of one magnet
will repel the north pole of another.

Opposite poles pull toward each other.
They attract. The north pole of one magnet
will attract the south pole of another.

Earth Is a Magnet

Earth is a magnet. A big one! Just like other magnets, it has two poles. Earth's magnetic poles are not in exactly the same spots as the North and South Poles. But they're close.

South
magnetic
pole

Geographic
north pole

S
N

Geographic
south pole

North
magnetic
pole

How is Earth a magnet?
The rocks inside the planet are
made mostly of iron. The iron forms
a giant magnet.

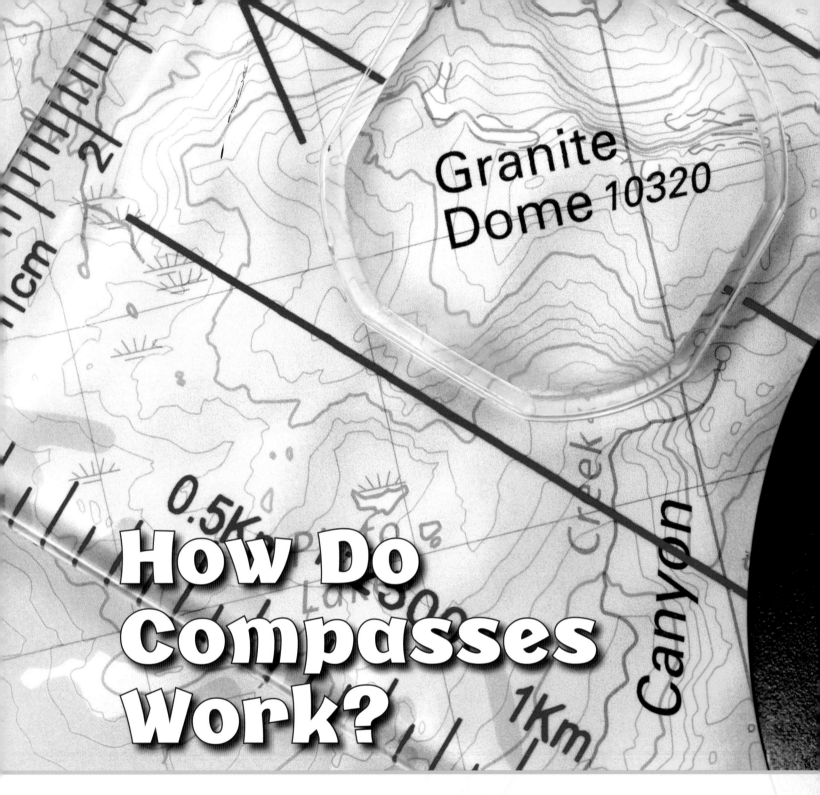

How Do Compasses Work?

A compass holds a needle. The needle is a magnet. Earth's magnetic power pulls the needle toward the North Pole. A compass needle always points north.

Compasses help people find their
way. They show direction. Sailors use
compasses to cross the ocean. Airplane
pilots and hikers use compasses too.

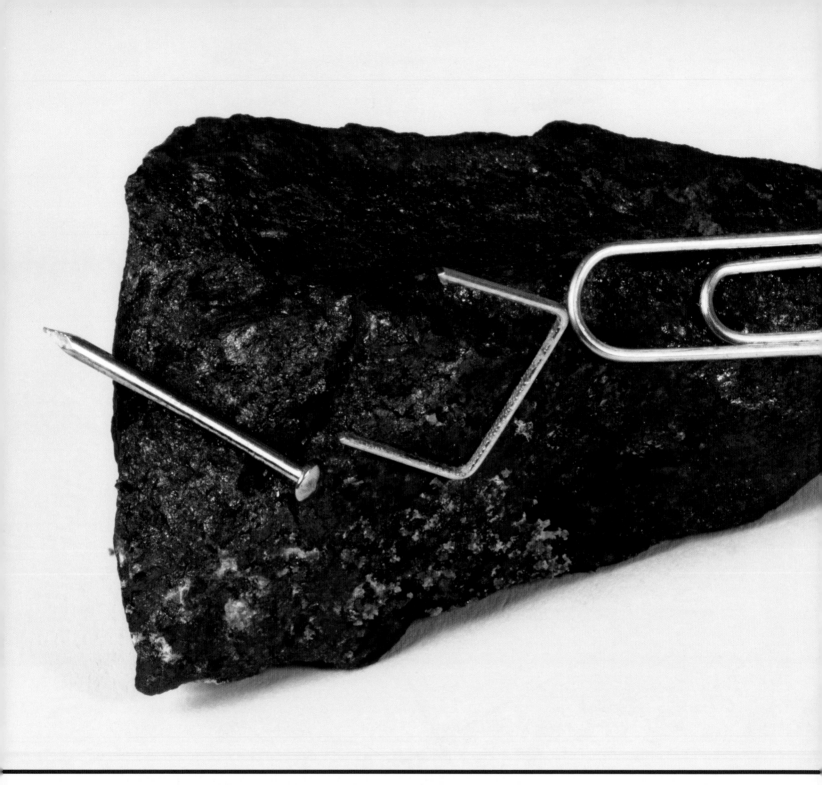

The first compasses were made from
magnetite. Magnetite is a black mineral.
It's a natural magnet. A piece of magnetite
is also called a lodestone.

Early Chinese compasses used lodestone.
They were carved into the shape of a spoon
and sat on a flat plate. The handle of the spoon
always pointed south.

Magnets All Around

Today we use magnets for many things.
Doctors use magnets to see where people are
hurt. An MRI machine holds a powerful magnet.
It helps make pictures of the inside of a body.

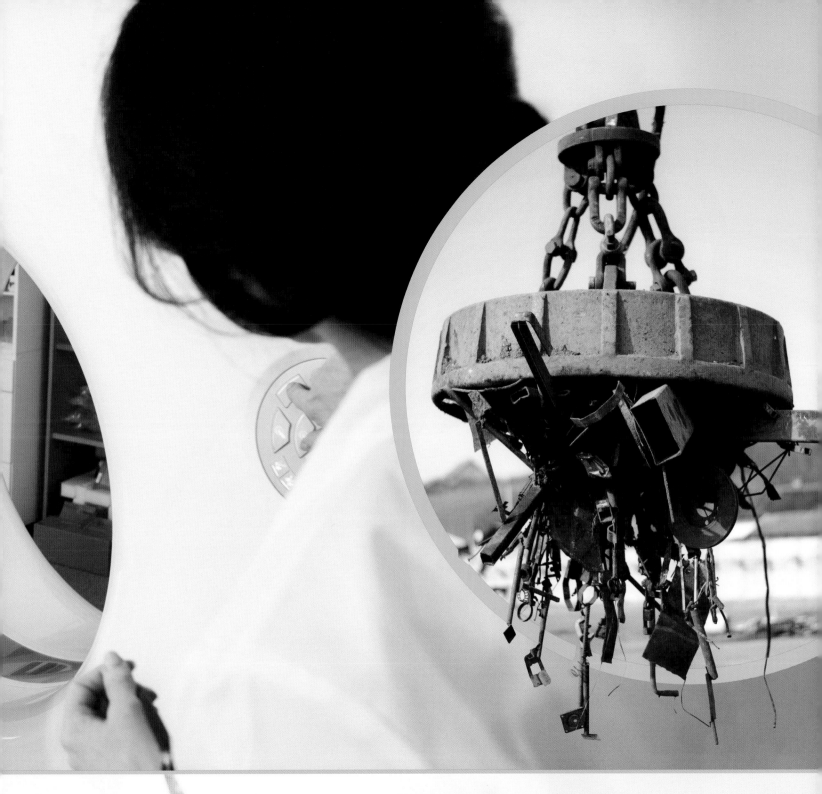

Magnets help junkyard workers lift tons of metal. The huge magnets move cars as if they were toys!

Fans spin. Refrigerators hum. Burglar alarms ring.
None of these things can work without magnets.
Neither can TVs, radios, or phones!

Magnets hold up pictures. They hold up
signs. Credit cards use magnets to help
people buy things.

The world would be very different without magnets.

Magnets make our lives easier and safer.
They make our lives more fun too!

Move It with Magnets!

Magnets move things made of steel. This activity will show you how magnetism works through plastic and water.

What You Need:

1 x 1 inch
  (2.5 x 2.5 centimeters)
  square of thin green plastic
scissors

a stapler
a large plastic cup
water
a magnet

What You Do:

- Cut out a turtle shape from the plastic. Use the stapler to put a staple in the middle of the plastic.
- Fill the plastic cup half full with water.
- Gently lay the turtle in the water so it floats.
- Hold the cup in one hand. Drag the magnet on the outside of the cup to move the turtle.
- Can you make your turtle move forward and backward? Try using the magnet to make your turtle spin. Drag the magnet down the side of the cup to make your turtle dive. Drag the magnet up the cup to make the turtle climb out of the water.

- What other ways can you move your turtle with a magnet? If your turtle does not move, use a stronger magnet or less water.

29

GLOSSARY

attract—to pull something toward something else

carve—to cut a piece of wood, stone, or other hard material into a particular shape

compass—a tool that shows the direction of the North Pole

invisible—something you cannot see

junkyard—an area used to collect, store, and sometimes sell materials that have been thrown away

magnetic field—the area around a magnet that has the power to attract other metals, usually iron or steel

opposite—facing or moving in the other direction

pilot—a person who flies a jet or plane

repel—to push something away

sailor—a person who works as a member of the crew on a ship or boat

READ MORE

Adler, David A. *Magnets Push, Magnets Pull.* New York: Holiday House, 2017.

Dunne, Abbie. *Magnetism.* Physical Science. North Mankato, Minn.: Capstone Press, 2017.

Royston, Angela. *All About Magnetism.* All About Science. Chicago: Heinemann Raintree, 2016.

INTERNET SITES

FactHound offers a safe, fun way to find Internet sites related to this book.

All of the sites on FactHound have been researched by our staff.

Here's all you do:

Visit *www.facthound.com*

Type in this code: 9781515770831

 Check out projects, games and lots more at
www.capstonekids.com

CRITICAL THINKING QUESTIONS

1. Name two types of metal that magnets can move.
2. Sailors, airplane pilots, and hikers all use compasses. What is a compass? Hint: Use your glossary for help!
3. Magnets are used for many things. They are in fans, refrigerators, and TVs. How many of the things listed in this book can you find in your house?

INDEX